Acknowledgments

For almost 20 years I have had the privilege of teaching *Awareness Through Movement*, developed by Dr. Moshe Feldenkrais. This series demonstrates variations on lessons that were introduced to me by the trainers and assistant trainers in the Delman & Questel Feldenkrais Practitioner training program.

Through his work Dr. Feldenkrais sought "to make the impossible possible, the possible easy and the easy elegant." A special thank you goes to Susan Warren Warshow, founder and director of the Dynamic Emotion Focused Therapy Institute. Your personal and therapeutic presence personifies ease, elegance and possibility. This coming together of my passions, Feldenkrais and psychotherapy, would not exist without your influence.

Description

Authentic connection is a state of being that can be deepened through spontaneous expressions involving physical movement. Infant and animal behaviors demonstrate that reading and responding organically to and through non-verbal communication is natural to all of us. Physical habits and muscular holding patterns developed over time, however, can impact access to a free and easy exchange of these non-verbal behaviors.

Psychotherapy research suggests that well attuned non-verbal communication on the part of the therapist, including perception of and expression through facial movements, gestures and body positions, can enhance the therapeutic alliance and contribute to improved outcomes including the "re-wiring" of attachment patterns and enhanced functioning of the client's own internal regulating system.

How can therapists raise their awareness of physical responses in both themselves and their clients and allow for reciprocal and therapeutically effective non-verbal communication?

This transcript is meant to accompany the Anatomy of Attunement audio series. The audio series consists of five **Feldenkrais Method**® *Awareness Through Movement*® Lessons designed to stimulate the neural substrate required for effective non-verbal engagement (via movement explorations involving the muscles of the face, spine and breathing apparatus) toward the goal of corrective relational experiences in therapy.

Table of Contents

I. Introduction

"We have a brain and a brain cord. Our brain cord connects our brain to our heart and that's how our mind and body are connected"
---Jackson, age 5

When my son was about 5 he demonstrated the mind/body connection to me with a crayon and a piece of paper. He told me as he drew that we have a brain and a brain cord and that our brain cord connects our brain to our heart and that's how our mind and body are connected.

I happened to be working on a talk about relationships at the time so asked him how he imagined two people connect to each other. To which he responded, "Oh Mommy! Through our hearts."

I mention this because I don't see myself as having anything to teach you that you didn't already show up on the planet knowing very well. Mind and body connection within ourselves and heart to heart connection between us is our natural state. When everything that would interfere with either is out of our way that is where we naturally live and how we ideally communicate.

That said there are things that get in our way---that keep what is natural to us from being our normal way of functioning. Habitual and automatic patterns of moving and thinking and blind spots in self-awareness limit the ways in which we can fully experience and organically respond to ourselves and others.

An everyday example of this is the way in which many people find themselves sitting in their desk chair. No one wants to be all hunched over or in the variety of gravity defying positions we often find ourselves in. But oddly enough it generally doesn't occur to the adult brain and body to actively seek and achieve a better state---until after pain sets in.

This is not the case for young children who have not yet been taught to "sit still" and prioritize external forces, or "pay attention" as we tell them. They have not yet learned to disregard valuable, real time information and impulses from their own bodies. They have not yet learned to tune out a felt, dynamic relationship to their environment. This is the relationship these lessons seek to recover. One in which paying attention to the outside happens through (rather than at the cost of) attention to the self.

The Feldenkrais method is a model of somatic education that uses gentle movement sequences to bring attention to parts of the body and mind that are currently outside of awareness. The lessons are designed to do this in a way that activates a curious and compassionate dialogue with the self----a dialogue that is more in line with our natural regard for internal experience and a dialogue through which more possibilities for effective action organically emerge. This is true whether that action is sitting in a desk chair or sitting across from a client attending to them fully through our thoughts, words and attuned movements of face and body.

The lessons in this series will explore movements of the eyes and body that are essential to: ease in the carriage of the head, suppleness in the facial muscles and freedom in the spine, limbs and breathing apparatus. These explorations seek to restore natural and optimal use of self in all action—including the non-verbal behaviors (like nodding, facial expressions, eye contact and vocalizations) that are associated with deepening relationship and positive outcomes in therapy.

It is recommended that you wear loose, comfortable clothes and find a quiet room in which to do the lessons. Before beginning make sure you have access to both a firm chair and a comfortable place on the floor (like a rug or blanket) where you can lie down and move freely.

As we work together, you will be directed to move slowly and gently because moving in this way will enable you to sense more. Your comfort is your first priority. If something doesn't feel right, find a way to make it work for you even if it means imagining a movement rather than actually doing it. There is an abundance of research that suggests the neurological benefit to you will be the same. You'll actually benefit more by imagining a sequence than you would by forcing yourself to do something that is painful.

You'll notice I give you time to rest. This isn't so much because the movements are physically exhausting (although they can be), but because you need time to process the significant amount of sensory information being gathered. If I don't give you enough breaks, take more.

There is no video component to this series. Its important that you follow the instructions in whatever way you make sense of them. If you are attending to your comfort and only doing what is easy and feels good, you can't do anything wrong.

I suggest doing one lesson each day and extending your learning by noticing how insights gained in that day's movement exploration impacts your work with clients. Once you have completed the series you may wish to repeat lessons regularly. Since the richness of the work is in what you discover about yourself, you will find that a lesson can be repeated many times and continue to yield new and valuable results.

II. Lesson One

"Your hand is in front of your face, your elbow is out to the side, your shoulder is relaxed, and your palm is toward the ground, and then let your hand hang limply."

Turning the Head with Ease

In this lesson will be led through a series of movements turning to one side. At the end of this recording you may either start the recording again and explore these movements turning to the other side or you may choose to stay with any asymmetry you feel at the end of the lesson. This kind of asymmetry is a novel experience and will invite a heightened state of awareness. Any sense of unevenness you initially notice will dissipate shortly and what you may find is that the side that did not demonstrate immediate gains from the lesson, learns something from the other side.

Sit on a firm chair--a kitchen or dining room chair will work nicely or any chair that isn't very soft and doesn't rock or roll around.

Come to sit towards the middle or end of the chair so that your back is free from the backrest. Allow your hands to hang by your sides or rest them on your legs.

Turn your attention inward. Without changing anything for now, just notice how you chose to place your feet on the floor. Where are they in relationship to your knees and hips? Are they weighted and fully in contact with the floor? Is your sense at this moment that your feet play an active role in supporting you in a seated position? Bring your attention to your pelvis particularly the part of your pelvis you are sitting on. Can you feel the 2 bony surfaces under your butt muscles? This is why I suggest a firm chair. So you can feel your body, not just the padding of the chair. Are you sitting to the front or back of those bones--your ischium/sitting bones? Are you weighted more on one side than the other? Bring your attention to your spine---from your tailbone to the base of your skull. What I'm going to say next might sound like a strange suggestion, but give it a moment and see what comes to you. First, see if you can locate your spine just by sensing it (which is different than locating it by touch or sight), and then find out if you can make out the shape of your spine---again without touching or looking in a mirror or bringing to mind an x-ray you've seen---but just by sensing. We all know our spines curve, but what do you actually feel that tells you this is true? What direction is the curve in the lower back, how does it change toward your upper back? What is the direction of the curve in your neck? Notice your head and its relationship to your spine---does it feel forward of, behind or balanced directly on top of your spine?

Moving slowly and without going to a place of stretch or strain, turn and look in one direction and then in the other. Do this a couple of times. In which direction is it easier to turn? Easier may mean that you go further or that there is something about turning in one direction that is just more pleasurable at the moment.

Face forward and pause.

Choose one direction you'd like to improve for now---either turning right or turning left. And you are only going to turn in this direction for the rest of the recording. Throughout the lesson, I'll reference turning in the direction you have chosen. This is the direction. So turn now in the direction you have chosen to improve, and take note of a spot in the room that marks how far you can see easily when you turn in this direction at this point in the lesson. Once you've identified your spot, face forward once again.

Lift the shoulder on the side you have chosen to turn toward. Lift it just a little. And then lower it. Lift and lower the shoulder several times going slowly and not making the biggest movement you can make. If you have chosen to turn to the right for this lesson, you are lifting and lowering the right shoulder.

What do you notice as you lift and lower? Go slowly enough to notice the path the shoulder takes----is it straight up and down, is there a movement forward or back at the top or bottom of your comfortable range? Sense the shoulder blade sliding along the ribcage as you lift and lower? There's no bony connection back there between the shoulder blade and the ribs, just tissue. Can you feel that as you lift and lower? The bony connection is at the clavicle and sternum/the collarbone and breastbone. What happens there as you lift and lower? If you're not sure, you can use your other hand to check it out.

Lower the shoulder and rest for a moment.

Now bring your ear in the direction of your shoulder and back to neutral. If you have chosen to turn to the left, you are taking the left ear toward the left shoulder and away again many times. Stay within a range that is very comfortable. Imagine this is the first time you are moving your head and neck in this way. See if you can allow yourself to be very curious about this movement.

Notice the direction of your face. Do you stay facing forward or does your head turn as you lower your ear and bring it back to neutral? Is the movement of your head coordinated with your breath in any way? Do you breathe in when you lift and out when you lower, or perhaps the reverse or perhaps the movement is completely independent of your breathing. Just notice.

Rest.

Now put those movements together---bring your shoulder toward your ear and your ear toward your shoulder---so they each go in the direction of the other. But they don't have to reach each other. It's just a direction not a destination. And you're still working with the same ear and shoulder that you've been lifting and lowering. Can you allow this movement to be very easy? We can be so oriented toward doing something big or correct by some external standard. These lessons really are about cultivating and practicing an appreciation of curiosity, comfort and internal ease. This combined with developing awareness is where I believe the effectiveness of the work lies--as I don't believe either alone (awareness alone or the desire for comfort alone) is enough.

Are you tensing the muscles in your face or belly as you bring your ear and shoulder toward and away from each other? Do you need to? Does it help?

Pause with your head and shoulder at neutral. Take a moment and then turn in the direction you have chosen and find out if it's a little easier to turn in this direction now.

Sit back and rest against the chair. Where does your attention go when you rest? Can you direct it someplace else and just check out what's going on there? And then some place else? Noticing habits in how we direct our attention are just as important as noticing habits in how we move or hold our bodies. Moshe Feldenkrais said, "What I'm after isn't flexible bodies but flexible brains. What I'm after is to return each person to their human dignity."

Come back to the middle or front of your chair so you can have your feet on the floor and your back is free from the back of the chair. Take the hand that is opposite the side you are turning toward and bring it in front of your face. So if you have been turning to the left, put your right hand in front of your face. Bring your elbow out to the side, but keep your shoulder relaxed, turn your palm toward the ground and then let your hand hang limply. This lesson is actually called dead bird or dead crane. And this is why: Your hand is in front of your face, your elbow is out to the side, your shoulder is relaxed, and your palm is toward the ground and then let your hand hang limply.

Turn this whole unit: elbow, shoulder, arm, hand, head in the direction you have been turning and back to neutral several times. As you have been---go slowly and do only what is easy and comfortable. As I said in the introduction, moving in this way---slow and easy, will make it possible for you to sense more. Are you moving the arm and hand along the horizon as you turn or does your trajectory curve downward or upward as you progress through the movement? If your arm gets tired, you can pause, rest your arm and come back to the movement any time.

As you turn---are you aware of any tension in your face or jaw? How far through yourself can you feel the turning? Is it a movement that happens only in your head and shoulders? Can you feel your ribs moving as you turn? What's happening in your upper back? Are you aware of any holding in your belly or butt? If so, can you let that go? What's happening in your lower spine and hips?

Rest your arm for a moment.

Return to the position (limp hand in front of your face, elbow out to side and shoulder relaxed) and return to the movement. Turn to the side you have chosen and focus your attention on the movement in your hips. Can you feel that one hip and the corresponding knee move backward as you turn? And the other knee reaches forward? Can you exaggerate that a bit, make it a little bigger but still staying in a comfortable range, accentuating the movement backward of one hip and knee as you turn. How does this movement of the hips affect your turning?

Turn a few times more and notice what is happening in your eyes? Do they move with your head as you turn? Is it a smooth movement---the movement of the eyes? A few times take your eyes opposite your head as you turn. Go easy this is an unusual organization of the eyes and head. Turn once or twice more this whole unit in the direction you have chosen and take the eyes in this direction too as if there were something you wanted to see in that direction.

Bring your arm down. Come back to neutral so you're facing forward and rest against the back of the chair for just a moment.

Return to the middle or front of your chair so your feet are on the ground and your back is free. Let your hands hang by your sides or rest them in your lap. Turn one last time in the direction you've been turning. Can you see beyond the spot you identified in the beginning of the lesson? Turn to the other side. Turn one way and then the other way as you did when we started. What has changed? What differences do you notice in turning one way compared with the other right now?

Face forward. As you did in the beginning of the lesson just notice how you choose to place your feet on the floor now. How are you balanced on your sitting bones? What is your sense of your spine, the location and shape of it, your felt sense of it as a supporting structure? You may notice some differences in how you sense and how you are organized on one side compared to the other. Does one foot, sitting bone, side of your spine, shoulder, side of you neck feel different than the other? As I said in the beginning, you can repeat this lesson on the other side or just hang out with the differences and see what emerges.

Sit back, and rest against the back of the chair.

I began the series with dead bird because generally people report being aware of barriers to or limitations in moving the head freely at the beginning of the lesson. And they often report greater ease in the carriage and movement of the head after completing it. And that is one of the series objectives: ease in the carriage and movement of the head.

I also believe this lesson simply and easily demonstrates the bigger picture of what we can work toward in this series. If you can turn further or more easily now than you could when you began, and/or if you have a greater sense of being supported by your skeleton in sitting, this (in my mind) is mostly due to becoming aware of and involving more of yourself in ways that serve your intention and eliminating (perhaps heretofore) unconscious obstacles to doing what you do---in this instance sitting and turning with greater ease.

It might not have happened automatically that you involved your legs, hips, eyes and chest when you turned from side to side. Perhaps you experienced the involvement of those parts as positively influencing your turning during the lesson. Similarly, you may not have been aware that there was tension in your shoulder, or jaw or belly or someplace else that was getting in your way.

Bringing obstacles and options to the conscious mind is big part of this work, and a big part of moving, being and relating more fully.

Moshe Feldenkrais said, "If you know what you are doing, you can do what you want." We will continue to spend our time together carefully and compassionately making unconscious processes conscious through movement so you can better know what you are doing and more effectively do what you want.

III. Lesson Two

"Now relax your eyes, move from focusing on this spot or object to taking in a broader view, a panoramic view."

Converging and Diverging the Eyes

This lesson is based on an exploration lead by Russell Delman in the Delman and Questel Feldenkrais Practitioner Training in New York in 1995. Sit toward the middle or front of a firm chair so that your feet can easily reach the floor and so that your back is not resting against the back of the chair for now---unless you cannot be comfortable without the support of the chair behind you.

Take a moment to tune into your body---sensing the muscles in your face and neck noticing any signs of tension or holding. Sense your feet on the floor and your butt on the chair. In general how well supported do you feel by your feet, pelvis and spine? How would you describe your breathing at the moment?

Identify something in front of you, a spot on the wall or an object that isn't too far away that you would have to strain to see it, and focus on it. Really take in every detail of the object or spot or whatever you're looking at as if it were very important. What do you have to do with your eyes to look in this way? Don't change anything, just notice---when you hold this kind of focus, what happens in the muscles of your face and jaw, your forehead, your tongue, your neck and shoulders? Has your breathing shifted at all now that you are focusing in this way? Keep focusing. How might you describe your state of mind?

Close your eyes for a bit and imagine that your gaze is widening. It's as if the two eyes are relaxing away from each other slightly. It's just a tiny adjustment. Open your eyes and keep gazing in this way, not focusing, but as if taking in a broader view, a panoramic view. Imagine you are on the top of a mountain, at the ocean or wherever you want to be taking in an enormous view. What happens to the muscles of your face and jaw? How about---your forehead, your tongue, your neck and shoulders? How's your breathing? Keep softening your gaze. How might you describe your state of mind?

Return to a more narrow focus on the object or spot you chose, looking at it carefully seeing every detail. Are you aware of any tension, even micro contractions in your face, perhaps in the muscles around your eyes, your jaw, your neck, your breathing? If so, exaggerate whatever you notice…don't strain anywhere to do that, but make any tension or holding you notice bigger. More pronounced.

Exaggerating these muscular contractions in this way will amplify tension patterns linked with focusing the eyes that might otherwise be too subtle to register in your conscious mind. I'm sure you've been advised against asking fish about the water. That which is most familiar to us, what we do all the time (no matter how much it interferes with what we want to do and how we want to be) may continue to slip under our radar until we do something like this to bring the pattern into consciousness. Only then can we have some choice around what to do about it.

Broaden your gaze again, blink if you need to and soften your eyes, let them move away from each other slightly and notice any shifts in your body and breath. Can you exaggerate those shifts as well?

Relax your eyes for a moment. Blink. Sit against the back of your chair.

Susan Warshow teaches that therapists must actively use their peripheral vision to practice with maximum effectiveness. She points out that as we maintain eye contact with our clients and focus on what they are saying, we also need to take in their facial expressions and signals from their entire body, such as posture, gestures, and muscle tone. This expanded awareness is a natural capacity, but it requires the therapist be in a relaxed state, the result of attentiveness to our own internal well-being.

If you notice tension in your face, jaw, neck, eyes or breathing and perhaps even in your state of mind when you focus your eyes, how might that influence the way you take in valuable information in the form of non verbal cues from your client? How might this habitual holding impact organic, spontaneous responses through your own facial expressions, gesture, posture and so on?

Get up and walk around the room. Find another object or spot on which to focus. Take in the details, look at it very carefully as if it were very important, and then let the eyes diverge. Soften your gaze. Walk around again, find another object and go back and forth once or twice at your own pace----moving from a narrow focus to a soft gaze paying attention to the shifts you notice in mind and body as you do so. *If you'd like to continue to play with this now, pause the recording and join us for the conclusion of the lesson when you are ready.*

Return to your chair, sit with your back free from the backrest and close your eyes. Allow your eyes to soften and as if diverge slightly so that the right eye is slightly gazing to the right of center and the left eye to the left. It's a tiny shift. And your eyes are closed. See if you can soften the muscles of your face, neck, belly, butt, how's your breathing. Slowly open your eyes and find out---can you gently bring your eyes into focus without interfering with the softness you've created in the rest of yourself?

Rest against the back of your chair with your eyes open or closed.

I want to make sure one thing is clear so that no one thinks I'm suggesting you walk around like you're on the top of a mountain all the time or worse with a limp body and blurred vision. Being able to focus your eyes is very important. We need to be able to look closely, to examine things in detail at times. It's also true that we don't *always* need to hold our eyes in focus---and when we do need to focus our eyes, we don't necessarily need all the muscular work that may have become habitually associated with focusing them.

In all of these lessons we are exploring the possibility of doing *what* we want and need to do *when* we want and need to do it---and with the least amount of extraneous effort possible. So we can focus our eyes when we need to focus them, and use the least amount of effort necessary to do it. And when we don't need to use our eyes in this way, we can do something else instead.

When we work with the eyes we work with some of the oldest patterns in the brain. Be gentle with yourself if you continue to experiment with this today. Also, if you wear glasses or contacts, try taking them off next time you do the lesson and consider spending at least a part of each day--- when it is safe to do so without them. So don't drive without glasses if you need glasses! But if it is safe walk around your house or office without them between clients to give your eyes a break from being held in focus, then try it and see what you notice. David Webber has developed an entire Feldenkrais-based program for the eyes and he makes the valid point that contact and eye glass prescriptions are the only prescriptions we are given without any directions for how to use them.

Close your eyes if they are open. Rub your hands together quickly generating heat between them, and then place your palms over your eyes completely shutting out the light. Allow the muscles of your eyes to surrender completely and to be held and soothed by the warmth and your hands.

Bring your hands down to rest in your lap or hang by your side. As you did in the beginning of this lesson take a moment to tune into your body--- sensing the muscles in your face and neck noticing any signs of tension or holding. In general do you feel well supported by your spine, your pelvis on the chair and your feet on the floor? How would you describe your breathing at the moment? How has your overall sense of yourself been influenced by this lesson?

Slowly open your eyes if you haven't already, and let the light of the room come gently back in.

IV. Lesson Three

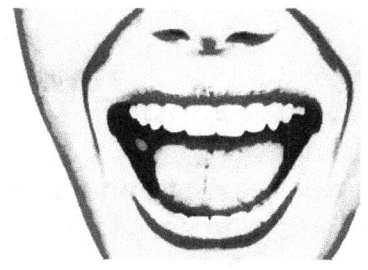

Freeing The Jaw and Tongue

Facial expression and vocal tone and prosody are important factors in attuned non-verbal communication. In this lesson we will explore the interconnectedness between the muscles of the jaw and the other muscles of the face as well as the throat and tongue toward the possibility of greater awareness, flexibility and organic expressiveness in the face and voice.

For this lesson you will need to have room to lie on the floor in addition to a firm chair. You may also want to wash your hands as you will be touching your face and mouth.

Begin by lying on the floor on your back with your legs and arms out long if this is comfortable for you. If you need something under your knees or to have your knees bent so that your feet are on the floor, that is fine. If you need something under your head, use a folded towel or blanket rather than a soft pillow which would inhibit freedom of movement. Pause the recording and get what you need, and begin again when you are ready.

Once you are comfortable on the floor, take a moment to bring your attention to your jaw. The jaw is actually separate from the rest of the skull, but we often don't experience it that way. What's your sense of this at the moment? The separateness of the jaw and the skull? What's your sense of the space in your mouth, the space between your teeth, how is your tongue resting in your mouth?

The position of the jaw reveals information about arousal and emotion. I'm sure you've notice clients clenching their jaw or felt it in yourself or you've seen or experienced a slight shifting forward of the jaw. Take a moment to just imagine---get a mental image of---these two expressions: the jaw clenching and a shifting of the jaw forward. What do they each communicate?

I'm going to give you time to experiment with activating the jaw muscles in these ways—clenching down and shifting forward. So go ahead and clench your jaw---be gentle though, don't strain anything to do it. Notice what happens in the other muscles of your face and neck. What about the space in your throat? Do you have more, or less, or the same space in your throat when you clench your jaw. Release it and clench again if you aren't sure. How about when you shift the jaw forward? What do you notice in the muscles of your eyes, face and neck? What happens to the space in your throat?

Clench your jaw again. What impact does this have on your breathing? Do you notice any shift related to your breath when you shift the jaw forward? Try it and find out.

What thoughts or emotions surface when you clench your jaw? How about when you shift it forward? Relax your jaw.

If you notice a readiness toward particular thoughts and/or emotions related to these two positions of the jaw, consider how unconscious holding in the jaw might affect flexibility in emotional state and spontaneity in emotional responsiveness to another.

Open and close your mouth slowly. It doesn't need to be a big movement. Repeat this movement many times, resting when you need to, and notice: is it only your jaw that moves up and down or does your head move up and down as well? See if you can allow this movement to occur in the jaw, and let the head rest for now. Continue to gently explore the movement of opening and closing the mouth and bring your hands to the back of your neck and check out what goes on there as you open an close. Pause the movement for a moment. Come back to opening and closing the mouth and move your hands to your face. Feel what happens in all the muscles of your face as you open and close. Take your time exploring----the forehead, temples, the area around your eyes, muscles of the jaw, the joints of the jaw. What do you with your tongue as you open and close?

Rest.

Slide your jaw forward so that your lower teeth move in front of your upper teeth slightly. And back again. Be gentle with this, slow and small. Repeat that movement several times—sliding the jaw forward and back to neutral.

What happens to your tongue? Do the other muscles of the face want to get involved? You can use your hands to check. Experiment with sliding the jaw forward and back while allowing the other muscles of the face to rest. Just don't invite them to the party. Can your breath be easy and uninterrupted by this movement---sliding the jaw forward and back.

Pause. Rest your hands by your sides if they aren't already. Is there a space between your upper and lower teeth as you rest? Swallow and feel what happens to that space? Open your jaw---get some space between your teeth. Can you swallow without your teeth touching? Without your jaw closing? Just notice. Can you engage the muscles of the throat without engaging the muscles of the jaw?

Reach your lips forward like you were going to kiss someone and then let the lips relax back. Do that movement a few times, reaching the lips and then relaxing them back. What do you do with your jaw as you reach your lips. Is it only your lips reaching or do you do something in your jaw and neck and other muscles of the face and tongue as well? What do you need to do in order to avoid over involving parts of yourself that you don't need to involve in order to reach the lips forward? Just play with it a bit. Let that go just pause for a moment.

Repeat the initial movement of opening and closing your mouth a few times. What do you notice in the muscles of the face, neck, tongue, throat, breath...?

Roll to your side slowly, come to stand and make your way to sit in a firm chair. Sit to toward the middle or front of the chair so that your back is free of the backrest if you can do this comfortably.

Open and close your mouth as you did when lying on the floor. How is it different in this position? Keep opening and closing gently and easily. Use your hands to explore the muscles of your face and neck as you do this. Notice if you tilt your head as you open and close?

Pause. Rest your hands on your lap or let them hang by your sides

Move your jaw forward and back so that the lower teeth move in front of the upper teeth and then back to neutral a few times. You may hear noises or feel sticky areas, be gentle with yourself as this may be the first time you've explored moving this joint in this way. What do you notice in your face, neck, tongue and throat? Can you allow yourself to be very curious about this movement---curious about how easy and effortless you can make it, curious about how you can involve only what you need to involve in order to move your jaw forward and back.

Stop the movement for a moment.

Take your jaw forward slightly once more and leave it there and then move it a little right and left. Use your hands to feel what happens in the TMJ---the jaw joints right in front of your ears, as you do this. Let your arms rest down, and continue to shift the jaw right and left. Rest when you need to. Does your tongue become activated? What about your lips? Do they need to? What do your eyes do as you shift your jaw right and left?

Pause the movement a moment.

Shift the jaw forward slightly again and resume the movement of shifting the jaw right and left, take your eyes with your jaw. So as your jaw goes to the right, your eyes look to the right. And then both jaw and eyes go left.

Now take your eyes in opposition. Can you do that without interfering with the ease and smoothness of the movement in the jaw?

Have your eyes stay oriented forward now and once or twice more shift the jaw right and left.

Before returning to the floor to rest, open and close your mouth a couple of times. What's that like now?

Return to lying on your back on the floor. Have your legs long---or bend them if you need to, and place the soles of your feet on the floor. Have only a firm support like a folded towel under your head if you need something there. Just rest for a moment.

Give yourself some space between your teeth---so let your jaw hang open slightly. Very gently begin to slide your tongue out of your mouth and in the direction of your chin only as far as it's comfortable, and then allow your tongue to slide back in to rest inside your mouth. Do this a few times sliding the tongue out towards your chin and allowing the tongue to slide back in. As you do this, pay attention to any activation in the muscles of the face, any tightening in the throat or holding of the breath. See if you can allow the face, the jaw and the throat to be quiet and the breath to be uninterrupted by the gentle reaching of the tongue out of the mouth towards the chin and the sliding of the tongue back to rest inside the mouth. I actually do just this movement often between clients. Never when sitting across from a client for obvious reasons, but between clients. And I generally notice a release in my jaw immediately as a result. You'll have to see for yourself what a mindful exploration of this movement does for you.

Let your tongue rest in your mouth.

Open and close your mouth. What happens in the muscles of your face, neck, tongue and throat? Has anything shifted since the beginning of the lesson.

Stop the movement. Notice how your jaw rests now. What is your sense of the space in your mouth, the space between the teeth, the space in your throat? How is your tongue resting in your mouth? What is your sense of your jaw as being separate from your skull now?

I had a voice teacher at Cal-Arts who made us pay her a dollar every time she saw us with our mouths closed. This was to encourage us to become aware of habitual patterns of holding in the jaw. I don't recommend walking around with your mouth hanging open or finding someone to punish you for closing it. But perhaps you can find a way to playfully check in with your jaw throughout the day today. And begin to pay attention to how holding there affects adjacent muscles of the face, neck, tongue and throat and the freedom of your breath and even your voice.

V. Lesson Four

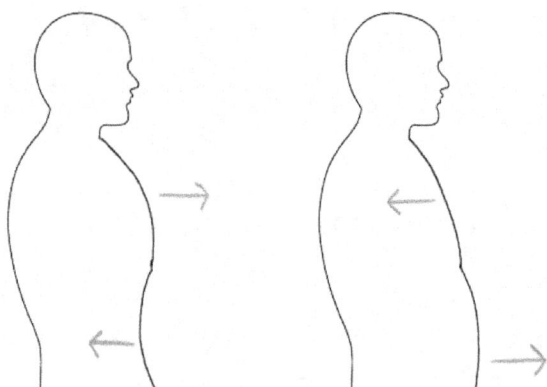

"Think of a long balloon ½ filled with air. It's as if you are pushing the air from one end of the balloon the other. Some people use the image of a see-saw to describe this movement."

See Saw Breathing

Lie on your back on the floor. If you need something under your head, use a folded towel or something comfortable but firm (not a squishy pillow).

I imagine I need to say very little about the role of breathing in signaling and regulating arousal levels. Recognizing shallow breathing, held breath, a big sigh, relaxed breathing (and so on) in ourselves and in our clients gives us important information about arousal, anxiety and availability for connection. Different models of therapy interpret and address these phenomena in different ways, and that won't be our focus here. Our focus will be on getting our radars tuned into our own internal experience of breathing.

I don't believe there is a correct way to breathe. So I won't be giving you instructions on how to breathe, but rather together we will be experimenting with allowing for expansion and flexibility in areas of the body that participate in breathing. This won't require any particular skill set or knowledge about breathing---just an open, curious mind through which you can newly explore something you do all day, everyday---something that impacts and communicates your state of mind, state of body and degree of readiness for relationship---your breathing.

Bend your knees and stand your feet on the floor hip distance apart and at a distance from your butt that allows your legs to feel securely supported.

Bring your attention to your breathing. Which parts of your body are active as you inhale (where do you feel movement as you breathe in)? Which parts of you are you aware of as you breathe out? If you had to describe your breathing as physical sensations alone, what might you say (i.e. I can feel my back press against the floor as I inhale, I can feel my belly tighten as I exhale, feel my throat open as I breathe in...)? What would you say? What is the depth, ease, satisfaction of your breathing right now?

Gently protrude your belly---as if you were inflating a balloon in your lower abdomen.

Allow your belly muscles to relax back to their normal resting position. Repeat this movement several times. Don't rock your pelvis as you push and release your belly. Think of your belly expanding in all directions--- front, sides, back. As you expand your belly, your diaphragm is moving downward.

Do the opposite movement---pull your belly in and puff out your chest. Relax and repeat this movement several times. When you do this movement, your diaphragm is moving upward.

Take a breath and hold it. While holding your breath, alternate between pushing out your belly and collapsing your chest and then pulling in your belly while inflating your chest. When you do this movement you are moving your diaphragm down and up. Exhale when you need to, and repeat: breathe in, hold your breath and alternate pushing out your belly/collapsing your chest and then pulling in your belly/expanding your chest.

Think of a long balloon ½ filled with air. It's as if you are pushing the air from one end of the balloon the other. Some people use the image of a see-saw to describe this movement. Make sure you rest and breathe when you need to, and return to the movement when you are ready.

Repeat the "see-saw" movement for 5 breaths. Breathe in, hold your breath, do the see-saw movement until you need to release the breath. Breathe out Breathe in again. Repeat 5 times.

Rest for a moment with your legs extended long (if this is comfortable), and just notice your breathing---which parts of you are you aware of as you breathe in and out. How much of yourself are you aware of being involved in breathing now? What's the depth, ease, and satisfaction of your breathing now?

If you can't be on your belly with your head turned to one side easily, just imagine you are in that position and follow along with the next set of instructions while remaining on your back.

If you are able, roll onto your belly and lie there with your head turned to the right. Your right arm is resting on the floor so that your elbow is bent and your hand is near your face, and your left arm is down along your side. If this position works for you. If not, do what you need to do to get comfortable.

Breathe in, hold your breath and make the same "see-saw" movement. As you push belly out, your lower back rises and as you expand your chest, your upper back rises. Repeat several times, breathing and resting when you need to. How does having the constraint of the floor against the front of you as opposed to the back of you affect the movement? Are there parts of you that come to life---that are easier to sense---because they are now pushing against this constraint? And perhaps there are parts of you that come to life for the opposite reason---because they are free from the constraint of the floor in this position.

Turn your head to the left and switch your arms so your left hand is near your face and your right arm is down along your side. Continue "see-saw breathing."

Roll onto your back and rest. Just notice your breathing---which parts of yourself are you aware of as you breathe in and out? How would you describe breathing in terms of the physical sensations that you are aware of now?

Come to sit in a firm chair, toward the front or middle of the chair so your feet are on the floor and your back is free from the backrest.

With one hand on your belly and one hand on your chest repeat the "see saw" movements in this position. Let your arms hang or rest your hands on your legs and continue. With your chest belly and back free from the floor, which parts of yourself can you feel participating in these movements and how? What occurs in your upper back?, your lower back?, the sides of your ribcage as you breathe? Let that movement go and just breathe normally. What's the depth, ease and satisfaction of your breathing now?

VI. Lesson Five

I've had clients say after lessons like this---I feel like this part of my body belongs to me in a way that I haven't been aware of until now.

A Gentle Touch Brings the Body to Life

I was speaking with a therapist recently who expressed some inhibition around impulses to mirror gestures being made by her clients. Maybe a client is touching his heart in a moment of self-compassion or raising a fist in anger, and the therapist feels her hand wanting to touch her own heart or feels moved to encourage the expression of the client's rage by gesturing with him. But her body just wasn't free to follow those impulses. I myself have become aware at times that I've been sitting very still in session (not in a way that feels organic or attuned) or I'll notice that I've been gripping the arms of my chair.

I began doing this lesson in the morning before seeing clients, and I often repeat pieces of it between clients. I find it makes a big difference in my overall physical responsiveness----how alive and responsive my body feels in session.

Sit on a firm chair. Sit toward the front or the middle of the chair so that your feet are on the floor and your back is free of the backrest.

As we have in previous lessons, take a moment to notice your sense of being supported in sitting by your feet on the floor, your pelvis, your spine. Tune in to your breathing. Not just how you usually breathe or what you know about your breathing, but---how do you know you are breathing right now? What sensations tell you that air is coming in and out of your body right now? How have you chosen to place your arms? Do you sense any differences between your right and left arm right now? Differences in weight, length, vitality? Which arm feels more ready to lift? If you were going to wave or reach out, with which hand would you do it? And how about your hands? What position are your hands resting or hanging in? Is one hand clearer, more available, easier to sense than the other?

Come to lie on the floor with your legs out long if that's ok position for you right now. If not, make sure you take care of yourself and adjust. If you need something under your head, use a folded towel or something comfortable but firm.

Bring your left hand to your left thigh and begin to explore the thigh with your hand. Reaching, stroking with your hand all over the thigh. Using the hand to explore as much of the thigh as you can comfortably reach. Front, sides, toward the back, wherever you can get to without straining. Which parts of your hand feel most sensitive to the texture of your clothes or skin, to the shape of your leg? Are you using both sides of the hand to touch and feel?

Bring your hand back to the floor and pause for a moment.

Reach your left hand to your left thigh again and begin rubbing your hand along your thigh broaden your exploration to include the right leg. So the territory you are exploring has expanded---left leg and right leg, stroking the thighs with a curious and pleasurable touch.

Rest for a moment. As we progress through this lesson, you'll notice a particular constraint. You'll be exploring one side of the body with the opposite hand. Within that constraint I invite you to give yourself freedom to linger where your interest is drawn, and to ignore my pacing and go at your own. People often forget about the pause button. If I ever go on before you are ready, exercise your power to press pause and play again when you are ready.

Bring your hand to your left thigh and once again broaden the area you are exploring to include now your belly, pelvis, waist and lower ribs on the right. So this is your area to explore for now---left thigh, right thigh, right side your belly, right side of your pelvis, all the way up to your lower ribs. Imagine you are touching these parts of yourself for the first time. Discovering this completely new, precious territory.

Rest.

Come back to the movement, begin curiously stroking the left thigh and once again, the territory expands---begin to explore all the ribs on the right---the middle and upper ribs too. Explore the front of the ribs, the side and back of the ribs wherever you can reach comfortably but just on the right. Take your time feeling each rib. Using all parts of your hand. It's your choice whether to continue to return to the left leg with each stroke or to linger in certain places that call your interest and attention.

Include the right armpit.

Include the whole right shoulder. Can you allow yourself to be fascinated by what you find there? When your hand is exploring your shoulder, you can allow the weight of your left arm to rest on your face. Go slowly enough to register the shifts in terrain as you move to and discover different parts of yourself with touch in this way. Take in the hard places, soft places, smooth surfaces, rough textures...whatever you notice.

Once you have stroked up from your left leg and investigated all surfaces of the right leg, belly on the right, ribs on the right, right armpit and right shoulder to your satisfaction, travel back down again to the left leg, staying in contact with the right side of yourself until you get there and rest your arm down by your side.

Bend your knees as you rest if this is more comfortable or turn onto your side and rest there if you need to.

Return to your back if you are not already there and return to the movement---this soft, attentive exploration of yourself, making your way from the left thigh all the way up to the right shoulder curiously caressing all the way. When you make it up to the right shoulder, broaden your area of exploration again and bring your left arm overhead to allow the hand to explore the floor above head. But only do this if it's easy for you. You can also leave your hand in contact with your shoulder and allow your arm to rest on your face and just imagine that you are extending your arm overhead onto the floor wherever you can reach comfortably. So either do it or imagine what it might be like to include the territory above head.

Find a way to bring your hand from overhead on the floor back toward your right shoulder. The hand is always in contact with something, never hanging in the air. It touches your shoulder until it touches the floor and then it touches the floor until it touches your shoulder again. Find the easiest, most pleasant path back to your body and then along the right side of your body making its way back to the floor down by your left side.

Repeat this journey a few times---your left hand travels from beside you on the left, onto the thighs, up the right side of your pelvis, ribs, arm pit, shoulder, let the weight of your arm fall onto your face, reach the hand to explore the floor overhead if you like, and then bring the hand back again to your right shoulder and along your right side all the way down to your left thigh and to the floor by your left side.

Rest. Notice any differences you feel between the two hands? What about between the two sides of your body? What impact has this directed attention and gentle touch had? What do you sense?

I'm going to be quiet for a moment while you repeat this exploration using your other hand to touch, caress, stroke, investigate, explore the opposite side of your body. You don't have to remember exactly what we did, and you don't need to take as much time. Your brain is primed for this experience and just a few repetitions is all that's needed. Just do whatever your body remembers and wants to do using your right hand and the left side of yourself.

Wherever you are in the process of exploring the left side with the right hand, bring that to a close and allow your hand to find its way back to the floor beside you on the right. Or pause the recording and continue when you are ready.

Rest in any position you like.

Come to your back if you aren't already there and bend both knees and put the soles of both feet on the floor. Cross your arms and place your right hand on your left thigh and your left hand on your right thigh. Begin to explore both sides of the body stroking, caressing with the opposite hand---right hand explores left side and left hand explores right side from legs to waist, belly, ribs, chest, armpits, shoulders and even extending both arms to rest on the floor overhead—IF that is comfortable. And the arms can uncross when they go above head so the right hand can be on the floor on the right and the left hand on the left and they cross again as they make their way back to your body. Go at your own pace. You can start at your thighs and gradually increase the territory you are covering or you can make continuous strokes from your thighs up the opposite side of your body to the floor and back again each time. Make this exploration your own. I'll give you some time.

Next time your arms are overhead (if you are bringing your arms overhead if not just imagine this...) let your arms rest on the floor above your head and lift your pelvis a little. Remember your knees are bent and the soles of your feet are on the floor. What happens in your shoulders arms and neck when you lift your pelvis a little? Lower your pelvis and bring both arms back down by your sides, returning in the same way---each hand keeping in contact with the opposite side of your body. And repeat this whole sequence a couple times more---arms cross and stroke from thighs to the floor above head and back again, lifting your pelvis when bringing the arms overhead---IF that is pleasurable. Play with the timing of the lift. How can lifting your pelvis make it easier for the arms to meet or rest on the floor?

You can pause the recording if you need more time with this. Come to rest on your back with your arms by your sides, lengthen your legs out long, and just sense yourself and any resonating effect of the touch and movement. I won't suggest what to look for. Just see what you notice.

Take your time to roll to one side and come back to sit in your chair. Sit towards the middle or front of your chair. Feel the support of your skeleton, check in with your breathing, your overall state of being in touch with your body right now. How does your body know that it has been touched. What do you feel that tells you this gentle, stroking exploration has occurred?

Notice your arms and hands, where and how you choose to rest them, any differences you notice between the two of them. What if anything has shifted since the beginning of the lesson? "I don't notice anything" is never a wrong answer, by the way. "Nothing" is a valid response if it's what you notice. Differences that one might notice can be in position---are you resting or hanging your hands in a different place now than you did at the beginning of the lesson. Differences can be in muscle tension are the hands looser or tighter now than they were. Differences can also exist in how clearly you can sense them, how present and available they feel to you. Maybe there has been a shift in temperature (they're warmer or colder) or overall aliveness of the hands. I've had clients say after lessons like this---I feel like this part of my body belongs to me in a way that I haven't been aware of until now.

Either with one hand or two---repeat what you just did on your back but now sitting in your chair. If you need to be more toward the front of your chair to do and enjoy this, then adjust in whatever way you need to. Begin with your hands on opposite thighs---so right hand on left thigh and left hand on right. And explore your whole body as you have been---you can extend the exploration all the way down your legs to your feet and then all the way up to your face and head including the sides, back and top of your head---using a gentle, soothing stroke throughout and keeping your arms crossed so the left hand always touches the right side and the right hand always strokes the left.

Take as long as you like with this now, and consider returning to it, even just a moment of it, it every so often between clients throughout your day today.

Bridget Quebodeaux, MA, GCFP, MFTI has been a Feldenkrais Awareness Through Movement teacher since 1996 and a certified Feldenkrais Practitioner since 1998. She is a Marriage and Family Therapy Registered Intern (#74660) under the supervision of Anne Galbraith (LMFT #40830). Bridget sees adults (individuals and couples) in West Los Angeles.

Bridget teaches classes on mindfulness and movement for the general public and mental health professionals. She has presented her work to students at USC, Pepperdine University and the AAMFT Student Conference and to interns and trainees at Los Angeles mental health clinics including OPICA and Edleman Westside Mental Health.

Bridget has completed over 4 years of training in Dynamic Emotion Focused Therapy (DEFT). She has completed Pat Ogden's Sensorimotor Psychotherapy training for the treatment of trauma and a training in Psychosynthesis through Psychosynthesis Palo Alto. She also completed a year of study with Stan Tatkin in Psychobiological Approach to Couple Therapy (PACT) and has recently rejoined the PACT professional training.

www.ingramcontent.com/pod-product-compliance
Lightning Source LLC
Chambersburg PA
CBHW080356290526
45791CB00009BA/2894